D1539541

OFF TO THE RACES

PETER & NILDA SESSLER

The Rourke Press, Inc.
Vero Beach, Florida 32964

PHOTO CREDITS
© ARCA: pages 4, 7, 12, 19, 22; © Michigan International Speedway:
page 13; © Nazareth Speedway: page 21; © Pennzoil Company: cover;
© Peter Sessler: pages 6, 9, 10, 15, 16, 18; page 22 courtesy Daytona
International Speedway

EDITORIAL SERVICES:
Susan Albury

Library of Congress Cataloging-in-Publication Data

Sessler, Peter C., 1950-
   Stock cars / Peter Sessler, Nilda Sessler.
      p. cm. — (Off to the races)
   Includes index.
   Summary: Describes stock cars and stock car racing, covering such
aspects as the shape and nature of the track, seating of the spectators,
order in which the drivers line up, and use of flags.
   ISBN 1-57103-284-3
   1. Stock cars (Automobiles) Juvenile literature. 2. Stock car racing
Juvenile literature. [1. Stock cars (Automobiles) 2. Stock car racing.] I.
Sessler, Nilda, 1951- . II. Title. III. Series: Sessler, Peter C., 1950-   Off to
the races.
GV1029.9.S74S47 1999
796.72—dc21

                                                      99-13828
                                                      CIP

Printed in the USA

TABLE OF CONTENTS

◼◻ A LITTLE HISTORY

Stock car racing wasn't always as popular as it has grown to be.

A man named Bill France, Sr., who used to race stock cars and loved the sport, got all the track owners in the southern United States together in 1948. He told them, "I believe stock car racing can become a nationally recognized sport."

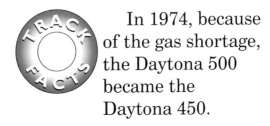 In 1974, because of the gas shortage, the Daytona 500 became the Daytona 450.

Stock car racing is now one of the most popular sports in America!

After that meeting they all decided to form the National Association for Stock Car Racing (NASCAR). The first Grand National race was held in 1949 and it was won by a Lincoln automobile.

This is Jeff Gordon in his Chevrolet Monte Carlo.

*Today's stock cars are all-out race cars that can go over
200 miles per hour.*

Mr. France's dream eventually became true
and today stock car racing is one of the most
popular sports in the USA!

▞ NASCAR

Stock car racing can be very complicated. In the early days of stock car racing it was very unsafe and a lot of the teams cheated by racing cars that gave them an unfair advantage.

NASCAR, however, changed all that. They set the rules that all race teams had to follow. NASCAR also said the cars had to be made stronger and safer, too. NASCAR also made sure the cars were **equal** (EEK wahl).

By making sure the cars were equal, racing is much more exciting. If one car won all the time, it certainly wouldn't be much fun to watch. With the cars being equal, it is the driver's skill that makes winning possible.

Besides NASCAR, there is the Automobile Racing Club of America (ARCA), which was founded in 1953. It, too, holds many stock car races around the country.

A race car can go faster if its shape is changed a little. NASCAR officials check the shape of every car before a race to make sure no one is cheating.

◼️◻️ SPONSORS (BROUGHT TO YOU BY...)

NASCAR and ARCA do everything they can to make stock car racing as inexpensive as possible. Despite this, it costs a lot of money to run a top team. It can cost millions of dollars. This is why stock cars have lots of **logos** (LO goz) and **decals** (DEE kalz) on them. All kinds of companies help to pay the cost of racing, and in return they get to put their logos on the car. The larger the logo, the more the company paid.

Without **sponsors** (SPON sirz), it is unlikely that any of the top teams could afford to race today.

 Jaguar is the only foreign car to win a top NASCAR race. It happened at Linden, NJ, in 1954.

Stock car racing is very expensive. That's why the cars are covered with sponsor's decals and logos. The sponsors help to pay for the cost of running the team.

11

ROUND AND ROUND WE GO!

Most stock car racing is done on oval tracks. The **spectators** (SPEK tay torz) can usually see the entire track from wherever they sit. This makes it is easy to follow the racing action. Some of the short tracks are paved while others are made of packed dirt. Racing on dirt tracks is very exciting because the cars slip and slide.

Stock cars race on paved tracks and on dirt tracks too, such as the one shown here. Racing on dirt tracks is messy but fun to watch.

This is a super speedway. It is called a tri-oval because of its three banked turns.

There are also the "super speedways." These are long, paved tracks, such as the Daytona Speedway. On these tracks the cars can reach speeds of over 200 miles per hour.

Stock cars also race on "road courses." These are tracks that resemble country roads with lots of curves, hills, and straights.

◼️ IT LOOKS LIKE STOCK—BUT IT'S NOT

In the early days of stock car racing, the cars were actually very close to being stock. That's because the people racing them couldn't afford to make many changes. Stock means the car is exactly how it came from the car dealer and has not been changed.

Today, the cars only look like the ones you can buy at the local car dealer. The car's body may look like a Ford, Chevrolet, or Pontiac, but underneath, they are made of steel tubing and steel panels according to the rules set by NASCAR and ARCA. They are called all-out race cars and cannot be driven on the street.

TRACK FACTS A stock car gets only 3-4 miles per gallon of gas.

Stock cars only look like the cars you can buy at the local car dealer. Underneath the body, they are completely different. The headlights aren't even real, they are decals!

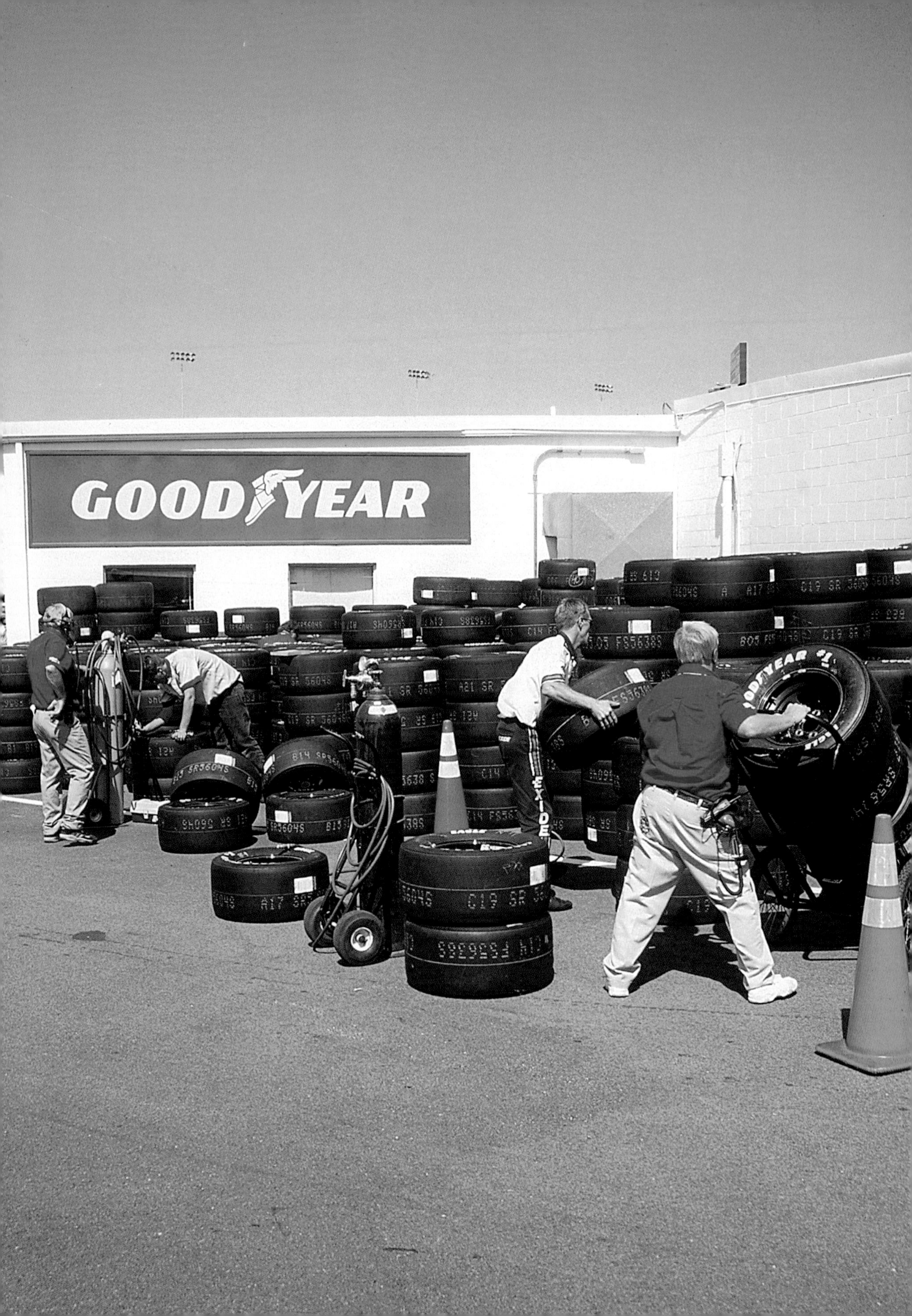
GOODYEAR

■■ ROLLING THUNDER

Stock car racers who race in the big national events have a very tough schedule. They go from track to track, racing two to four times a month for almost nine months.

They usually arrive at the track during midweek. This gives the drivers a chance to practice on the track. Before they can race, they have to **qualify** (KWA la fi) the car to see what position they'll start from. The faster the car qualifies, the further in front it can start. The best place to start from is the "pole" position, which is the inside left of the first row.

Stock cars never race in the rain and only use tires without treads called slicks.

Finally, the race day comes. The drivers line their cars up in the order they qualified and a pace car leads them slowly around the track. No one is allowed to pass the pace car. When the track officials see that everything is fine, the pace car pulls off the track and the starter waves the green flag. The race is on as all the cars floor the gas pedal at the same time! The noise is really loud and shakes your whole body!

The driver and his crew spend a lot of time practicing to make sure the car will run as fast as possible during the race.

The pit crew fills the gas tank and changes all four tires on this racer, and the faster, the better.

On some of the longer races, the cars have to come in to the pits to change tires and get more gas. If the pit crew takes too long, the driver can lose the race, but if they are faster than other pit crews, it can help the driver win the race.

Finally, the winner takes the checkered flag. The winner gets a trophy and prize money. At the end of the year, the driver who has won the most points is made champion.

 The most races won in a season by the same driver is 13. Richard Petty did it in 1975 and Jeff Gordon in 1998.

This is stock car racing at its best—when only a few feet separate the fastest cars from the slowest.

Winston
DAYTONA 500
1999
DAYTONA 500 CHAMPION
DWAY
DAYTONA
500
DUPONT
GMAC
PEPSI
ACDelco
DUPONT
AUTOMOTIVE
FINISHES
Hendrick

 GLOSSARY

decal (DEE kal) — design or picture prepared so that it can be attached to the cars

equal (EEK wahl) — the same in all respects

logo (LO go) — a letter, symbol, or sign used to represent an entire word or the name of a company

qualify (KWA la fi) — to get a starting position

spectators (SPEK tay torz) — people who watch

sponsors (SPON sirz) — a company that helps pay for a racing team

CONVERSION TABLE

200 miles per hour	322 kilometers per hour
3-4 miles per gallon	4.8-6.4 kilometers per gallon

A proud Jeff Gordon holds the winner's trophy of the 1999 Daytona 500.

■■ INDEX

FURTHER READING

Find out more about racing with these helpful books and organizations:

- George Sullivan, *Burnin' Rubber: Behind the Scenes in Stock Car Racing.* 1998
- Frank Moriarty, *The Encyclopedia of Stock Car Racing.* 1998
- *The Official NASCAR Handbook.* 1998
- Al Pearce & Bill Fleischman, *NASCAR Racing: The Ultimate Fan Guide.* 1996

- NASCAR's Official Site: www.nascar.com
- ARCA's Official Site: www.arca.com
- www.goracing.com
    Lots of information on all types of racing. The site also posts the results of every race.